Beginner's BALLOON Modelling

FUN KITS

TOP THAT! Kids™
Published by Top That! Publishing plc
Tide Mill Way, Woodbridge, Suffolk, IP12 1AP, UK
www.topthatpublishing.com
Copyright © 2004 Top That! Publishing plc
Top That! Kids is a Trademark of Top That! Publishing plc
All rights reserved

Getting Started

You'll be amazed at the different types of models you can make from balloons. Once you get to grips with the basic twists and turns, you'll be able to make all sorts – from cute ladybirds to snappy crocs – they're all in your fun-packed kit! So what are you waiting for? Get twisting!

In your pack you will find a selection of balloons, a balloon pump and several sticky eyes for you to peel off and use to add character to your models. This kit contains enough balloons to make all the models – but you may need to stock up on more in case you burst some, and you will also want some to practise with.

Top Tips

- Use the special balloon pump provided, fastening the end of the balloon onto the tip. Don't try to blow up the balloons with your mouth.

- Pump up the balloon until it is roughly the length stated in the instructions. Before you tie the end, allow a little of the air out. This makes the balloon easier to twist.

- To deflate a balloon, tie a knot in the end and ask an adult to snip a hole in the excess, leaving enough latex to tie a knot. Don't let go until the knot is secure!

- Don't throw away any odd bits of balloon – these can be used for the balloon scraps often needed to make noses and eyes for the models.

- Store this pack away when you have finished modelling, and keep it in a safe place away from very young children.

Round the Twist

To twist a balloon, pinch it in the right place with your fingers, and use your other hand to twist the end of the balloon round two or three times. You will notice that air gets pushed into the empty end of the balloon as you make more twists, so the balloon ends up at the right length to finish the model.

Lock Twist

① You'll use this twist a lot to make legs and bodies. Make one twist and slide your hand down the balloon – so that you can hold the first twist – then pinch the balloon to make a second twist. Repeat this so you have three twists.

② Bend the last bubble back and hold it with the middle bubble. Twist the two bubbles together so that they lock in place and don't unwind.

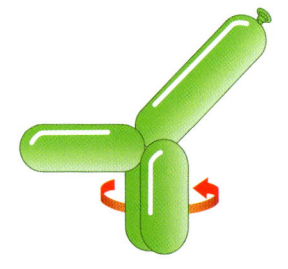

Ear Twist

① Make two twists using the measurements given for your chosen model.

② Bend the small middle bubble right over and double twist it at the point where it joins the first bubble.

Apple Twist

① Inflate a 3 cm bubble in a long balloon and tie a knot. Hold the bubble in one hand. With the first finger of your other hand, press the knot back inside the bubble.

② Push the knot all the way to the end of the bubble so that it touches the beginning of the deflated section, the 'stem'.

③ Grasp the knot through the wall of the bubble and remove your finger. To keep the knot in the stem of the balloon, double twist the new bubble.

④ Hold the stem and push the knot back into the bubble, where the air pressure inside the balloon will hold it tightly in position.

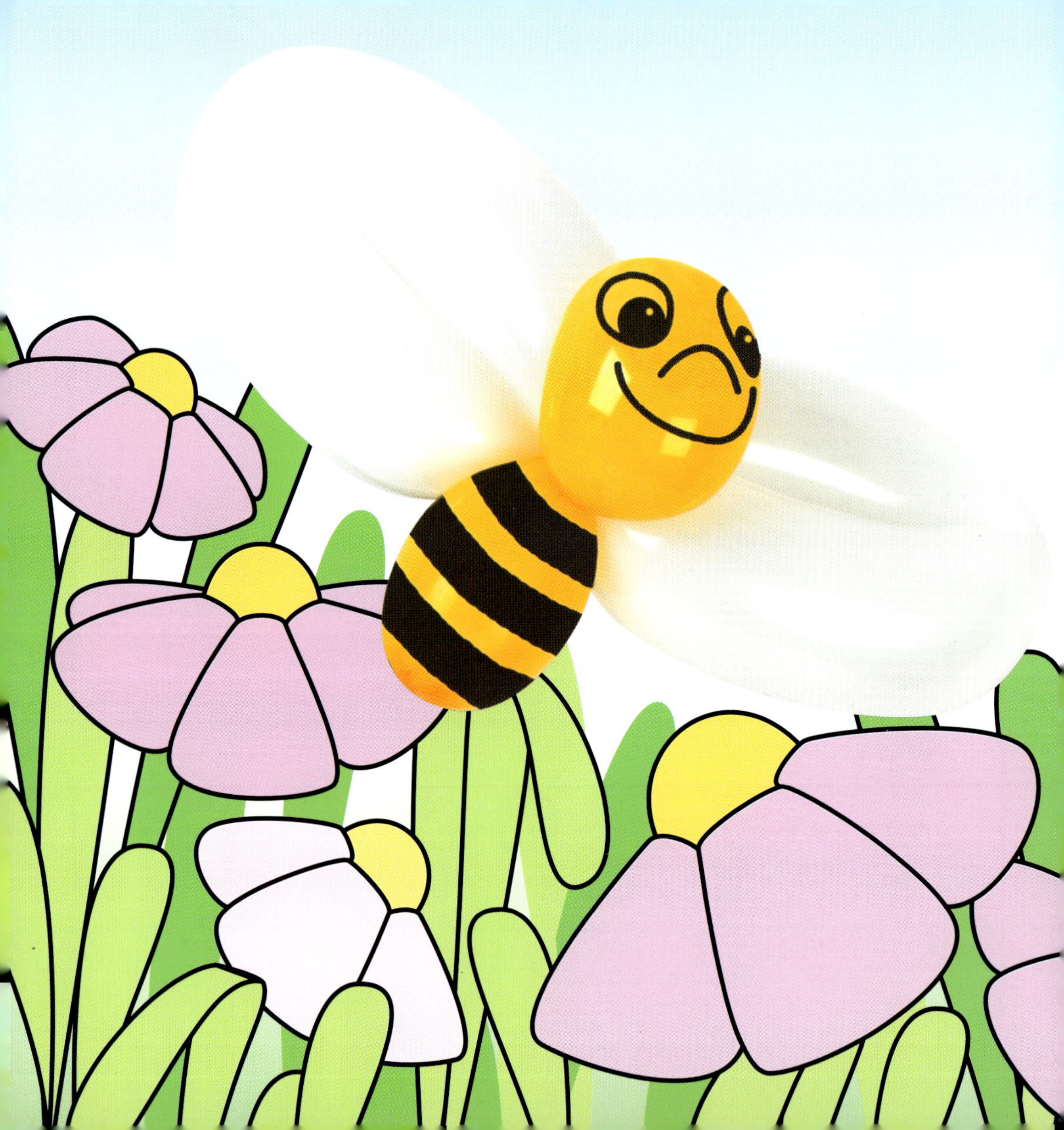

Buzzbee

You will need:
- two long balloons
- a marker pen

1 Half inflate one of the long balloons, tie and cut off the excess. Twist one 4 cm bubble from the end to form the head and one 5 cm bubble next to it for the body. Tie a knot at the end of the body to secure it.

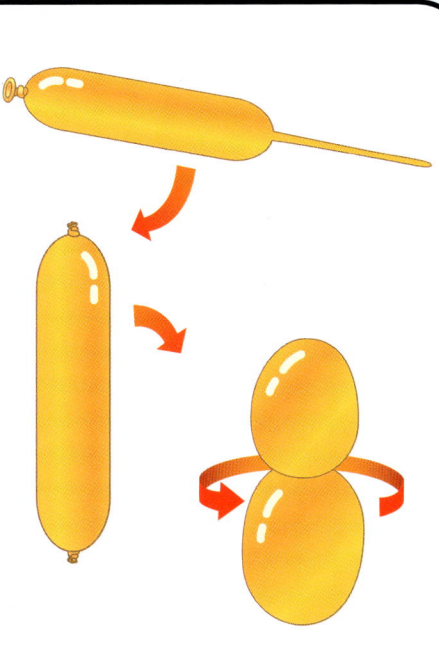

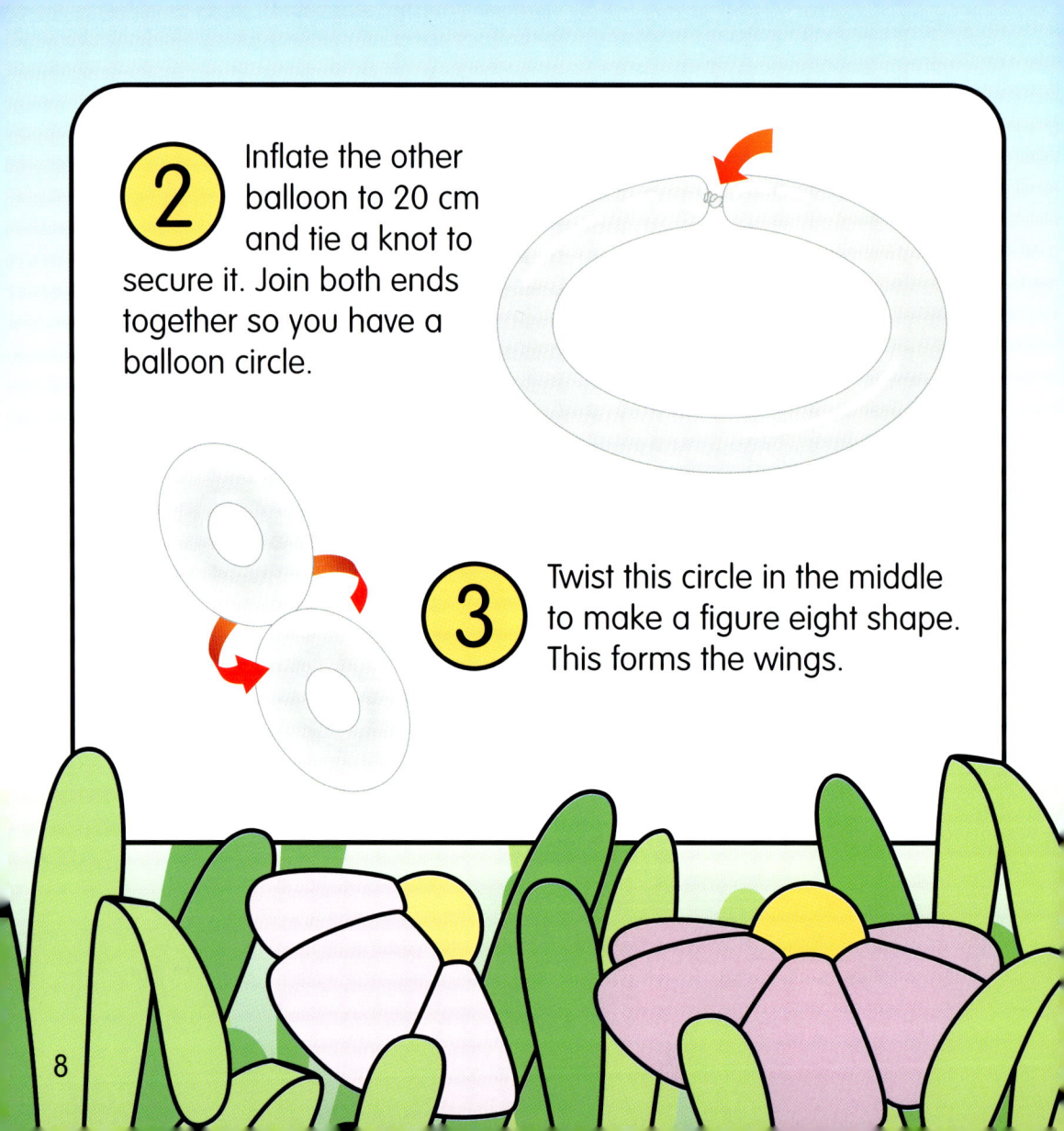

2 Inflate the other balloon to 20 cm and tie a knot to secure it. Join both ends together so you have a balloon circle.

3 Twist this circle in the middle to make a figure eight shape. This forms the wings.

4 Twist the wings around the neck of your bee.

5 Draw on the stripes and a face and Buzzbee will come to life!

10

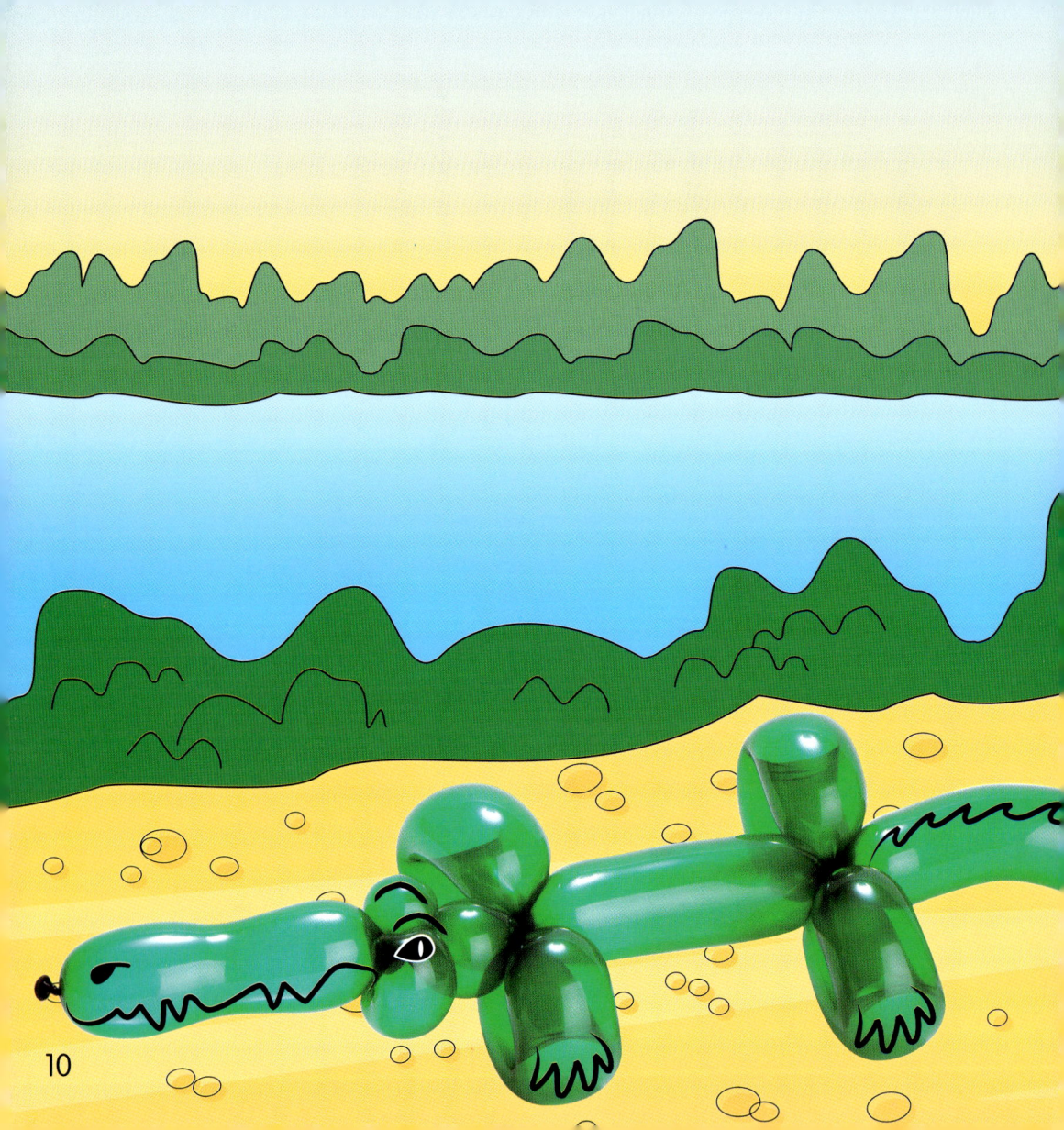

Doc the Croc

You will need:
- one long balloon
- a marker pen
- sticker eyes

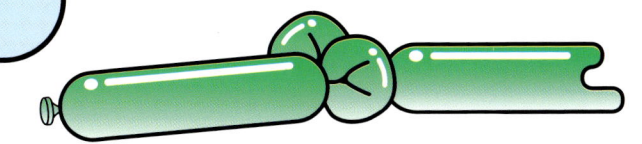

1 Inflate the balloon to 35 cm. Twist a 10 cm bubble from the knotted end for the face. Squeeze and twist a 5 cm bubble for one eye. Bend the eye bubble back and ear twist it to the head. Ear twist another 5 cm bubble for the second eye.

2 Squeeze and twist a 3 cm bubble for the neck. Twist a 15 cm bubble for the first leg. Bend this bubble over and ear twist it behind the neck.

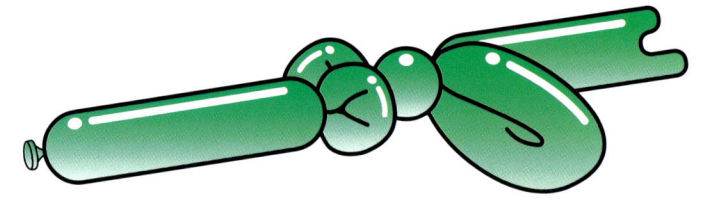

3 Now twist a second 15 cm leg bubble. Bend it over and ear twist it in the same place as the first so they sit side by side.

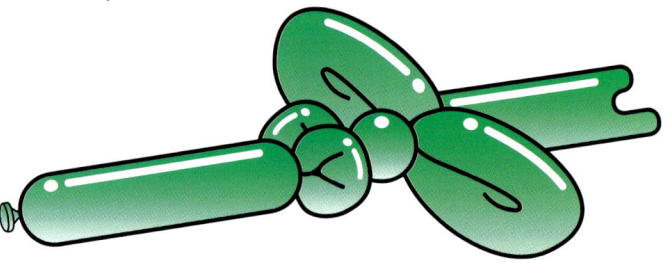

4 Twist a 10 cm bubble for the body and a 15 cm bubble for one back leg. Bend this over and ear twist it behind the body. Make another 15 cm bubble and ear twist it in the same way, to make the second leg. Straighten the legs to lie flat.

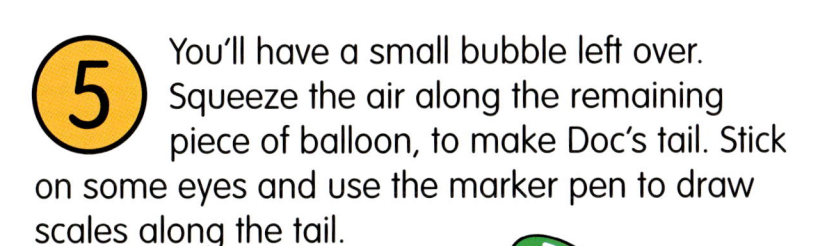

5 You'll have a small bubble left over. Squeeze the air along the remaining piece of balloon, to make Doc's tail. Stick on some eyes and use the marker pen to draw scales along the tail.

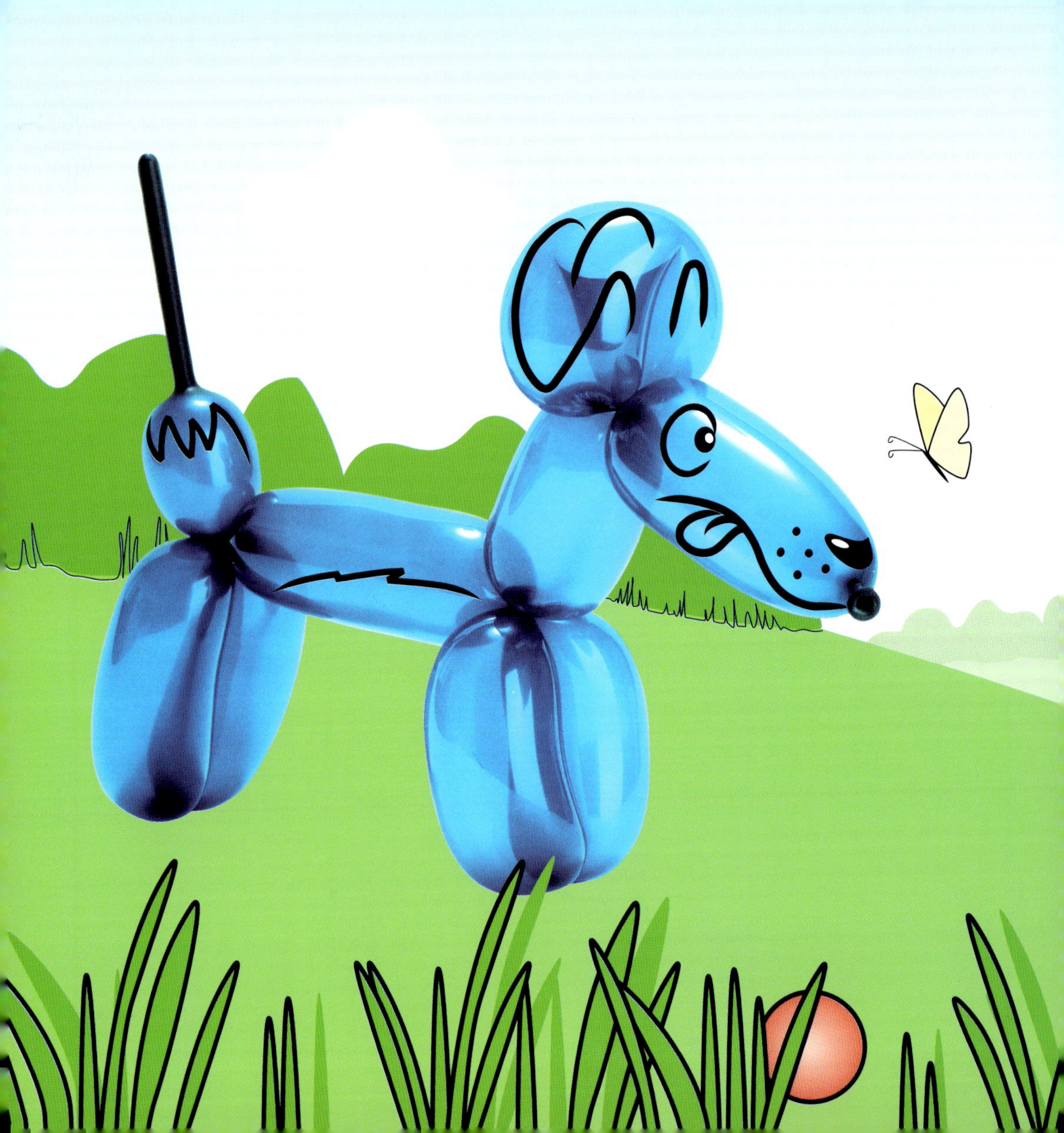

Perky Pup

You will need:
- one long balloon
- a marker pen

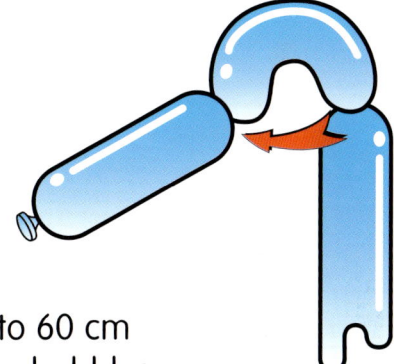

1 Inflate the balloon to 60 cm and make two 9 cm bubbles at the knotted end. Fold the second bubble over and ear twist it to make a nose and ears.

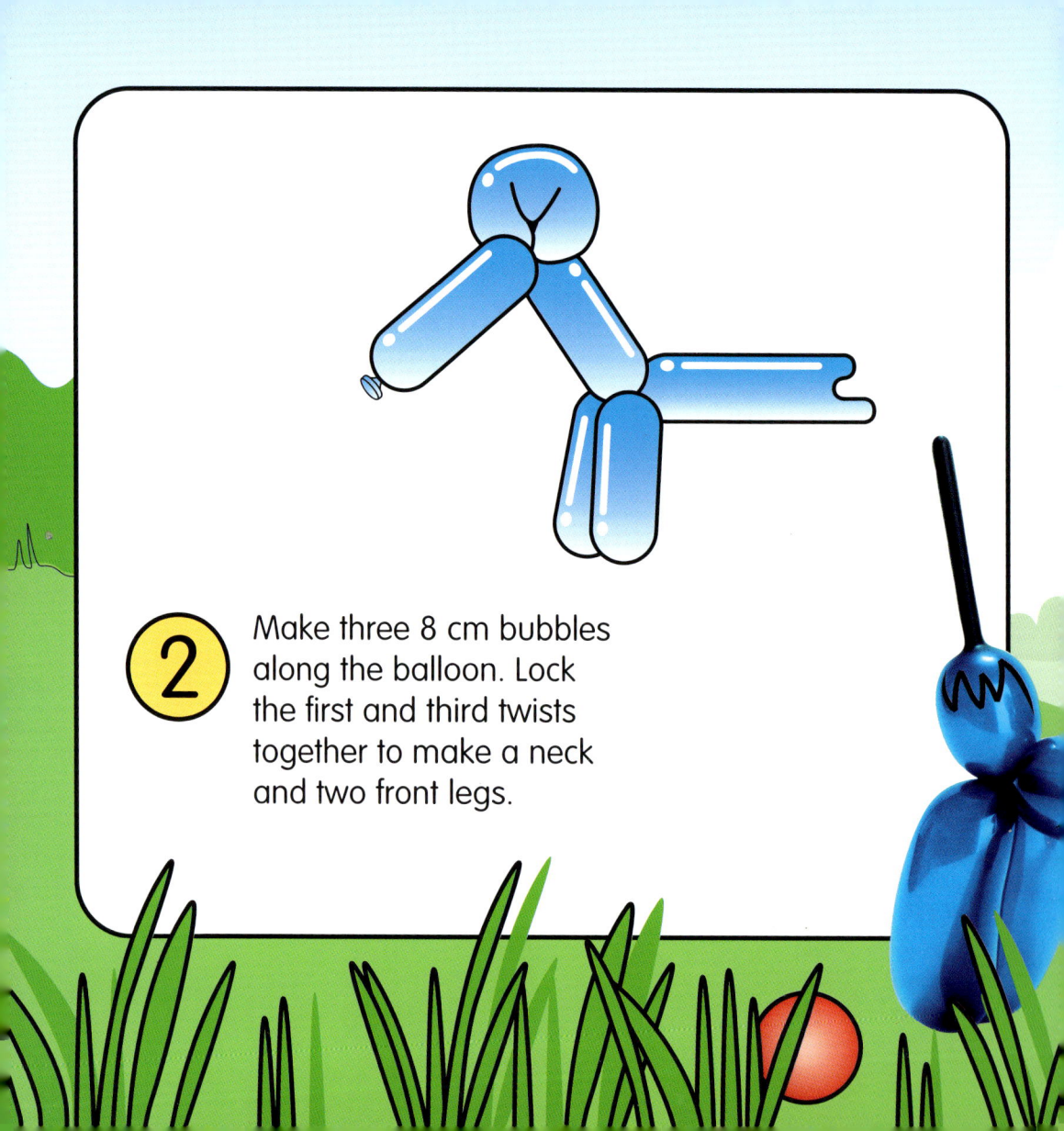

2 Make three 8 cm bubbles along the balloon. Lock the first and third twists together to make a neck and two front legs.

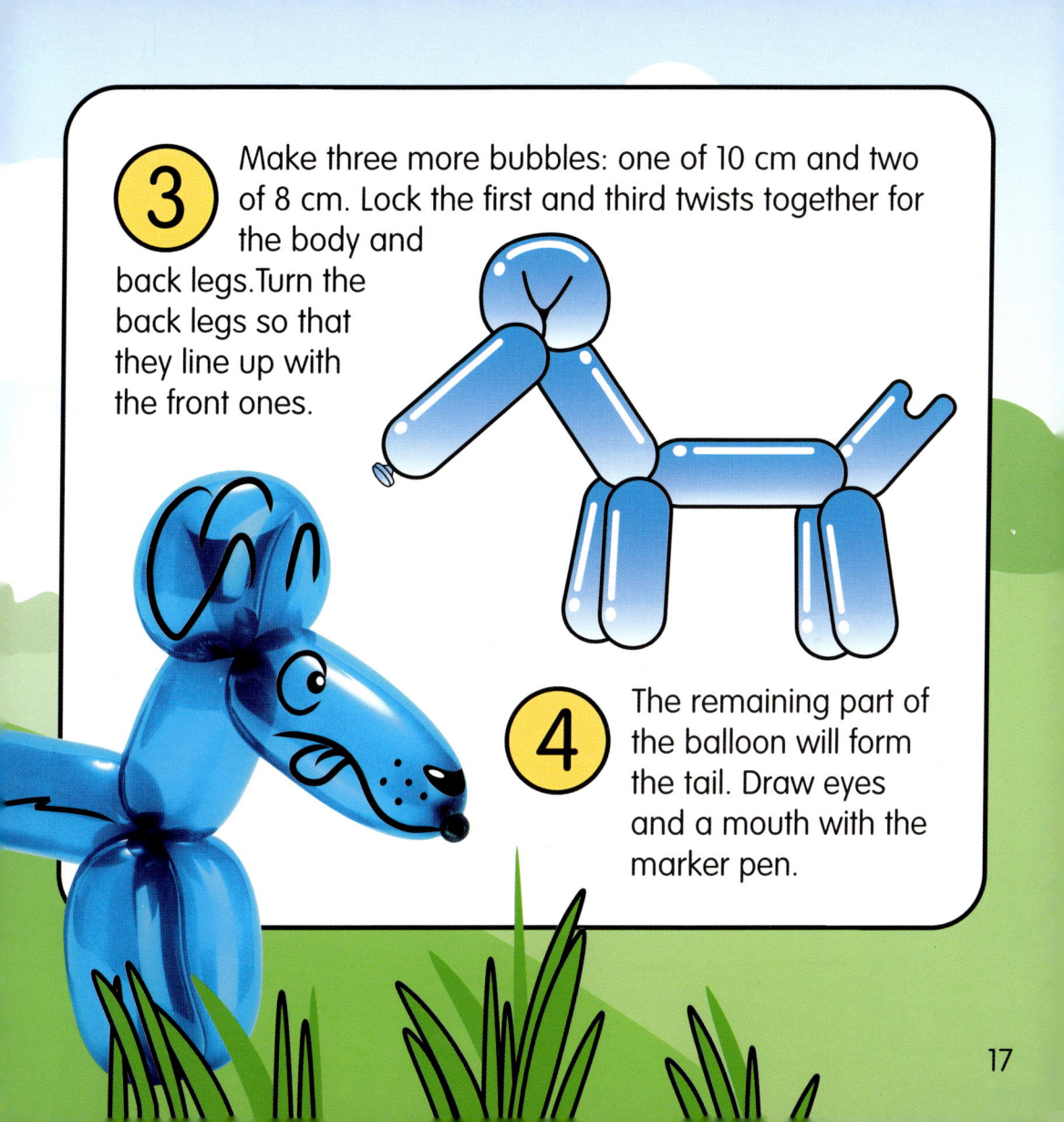

3 Make three more bubbles: one of 10 cm and two of 8 cm. Lock the first and third twists together for the body and back legs. Turn the back legs so that they line up with the front ones.

4 The remaining part of the balloon will form the tail. Draw eyes and a mouth with the marker pen.

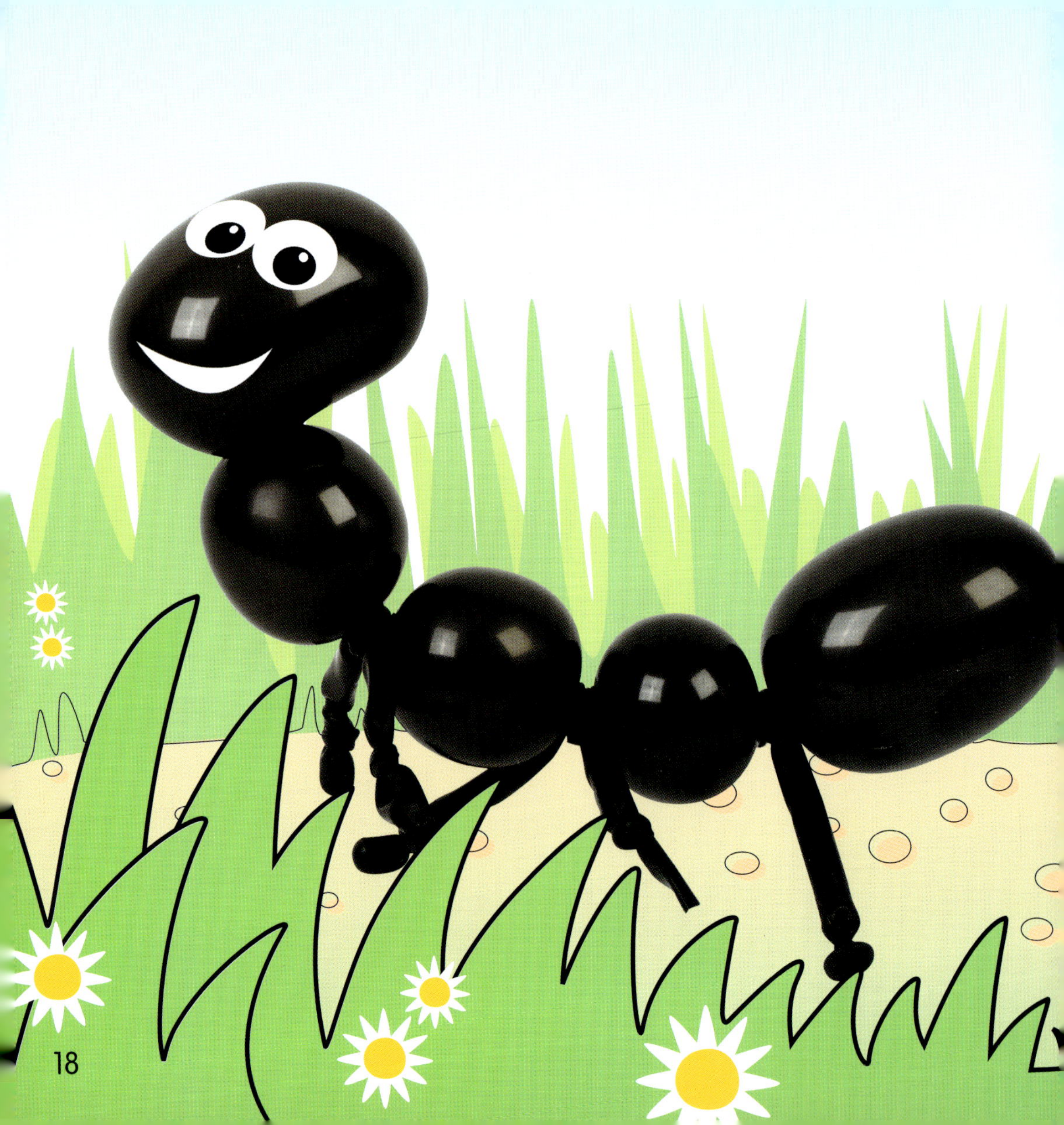

Ant-ony

You will need:
- one long balloon
- three balloon scraps
- sticker eyes

1. Inflate the long balloon leaving a 15 cm tip. Twist one 4 cm bubble for the head, as shown.

(2) Twist a 2 cm bubble for the first part of the body, then place one of the balloon scraps behind the body bubble, as shown.

3 Holding the scrap in place, twist another two 2 cm body bubbles behind it and place the scraps behind each body bubble. Twist a 3 cm bubble for the tail, then wrap the knot around your last twist. Finish with some sticker eyes.

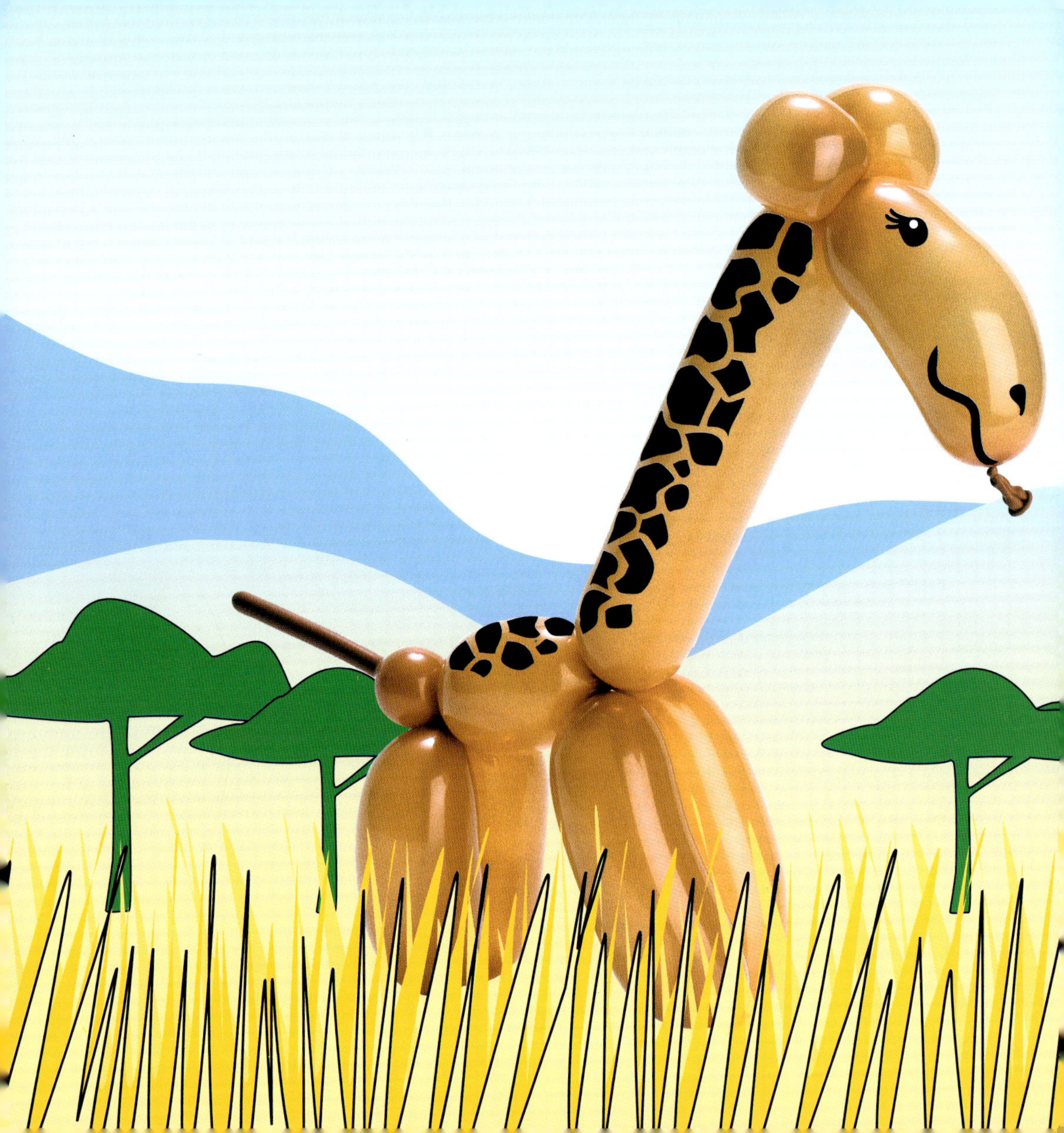

Geoff Giraffe

You will need:
- one long balloon
- a marker pen
- sticker eyes

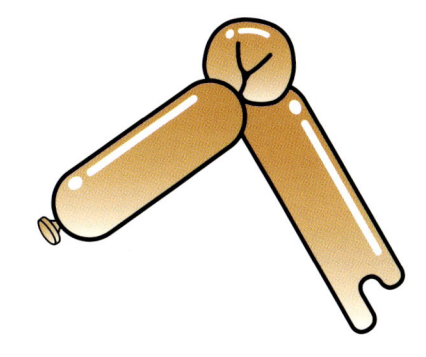

1 Inflate the balloon to 75 cm. Twist a 9 cm bubble at the knotted end for the head. Now twist a 4 cm bubble. Fold it back to the head and ear twist the two together.

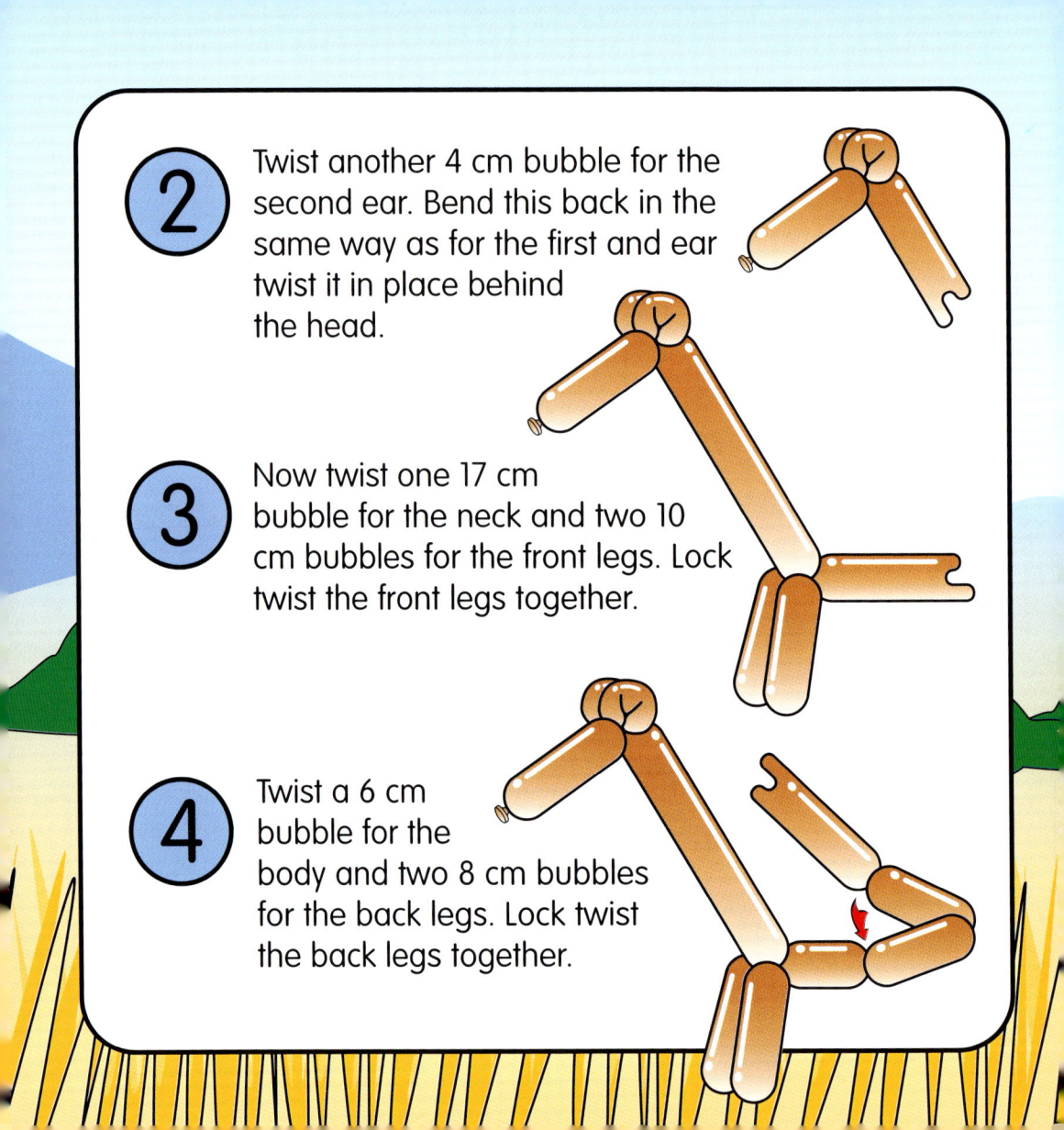

2 Twist another 4 cm bubble for the second ear. Bend this back in the same way as for the first and ear twist it in place behind the head.

3 Now twist one 17 cm bubble for the neck and two 10 cm bubbles for the front legs. Lock twist the front legs together.

4 Twist a 6 cm bubble for the body and two 8 cm bubbles for the back legs. Lock twist the back legs together.

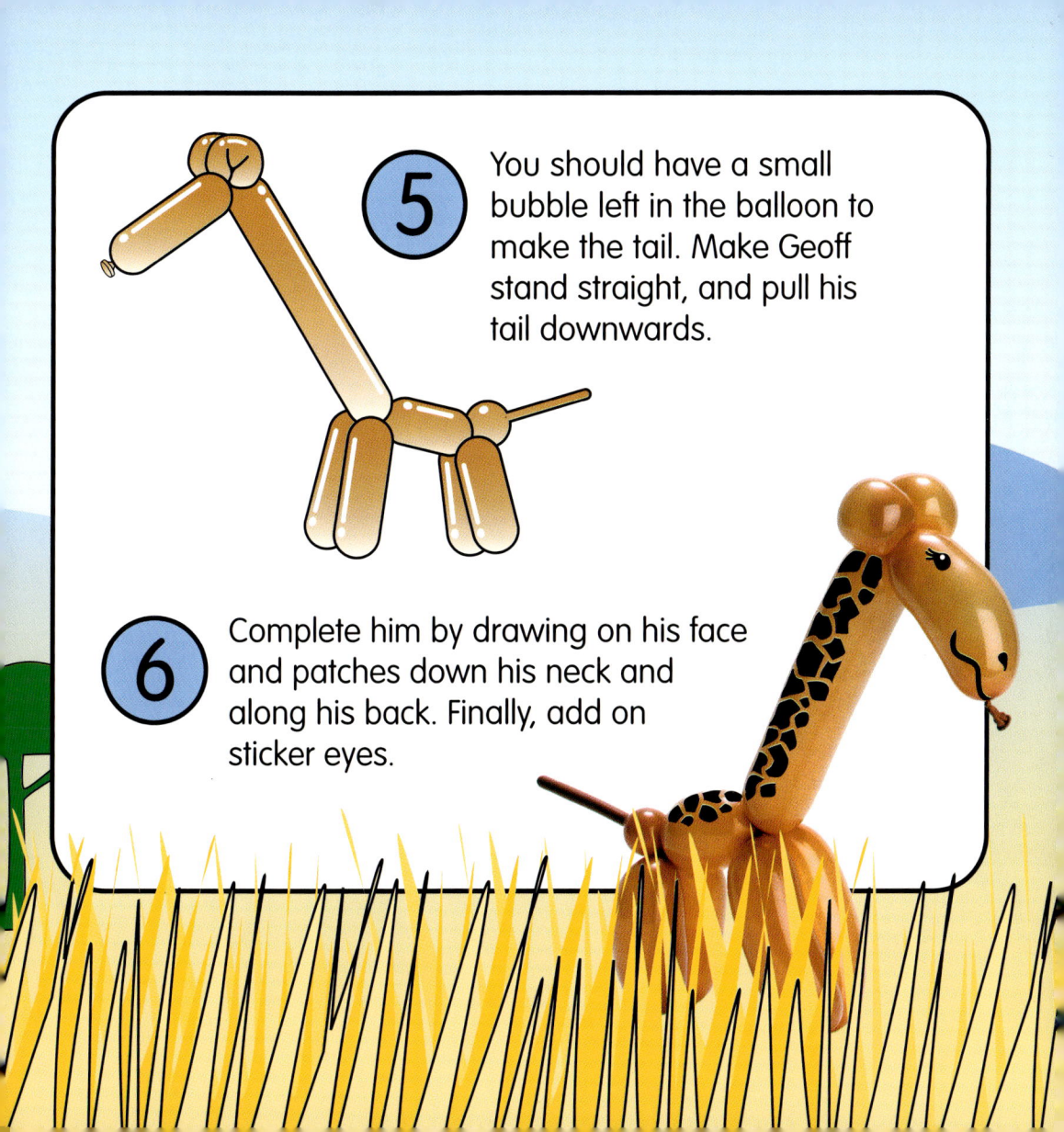

5 You should have a small bubble left in the balloon to make the tail. Make Geoff stand straight, and pull his tail downwards.

6 Complete him by drawing on his face and patches down his neck and along his back. Finally, add on sticker eyes.

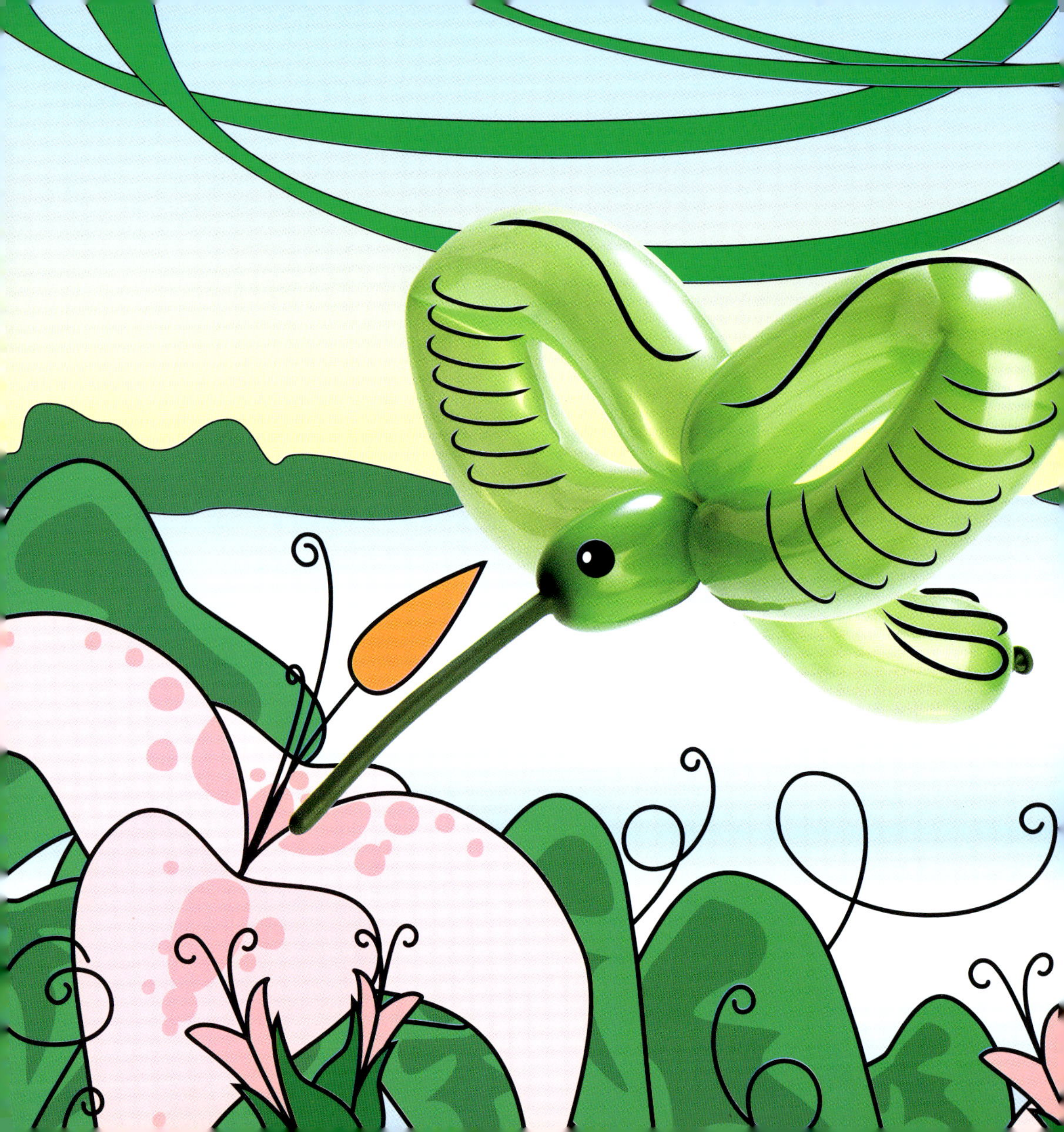

Hummingbird

You will need:
- one long balloon
- a marker pen

1 Inflate a long balloon to 80 cm. Twist one 5 cm bubble at the knotted end for the body, then one 6 cm bubble at the other end for the head. The long piece of uninflated balloon will form the beak.

2 Bend the middle bubble over and lock twist the head and tail together. This should give you a large loop.

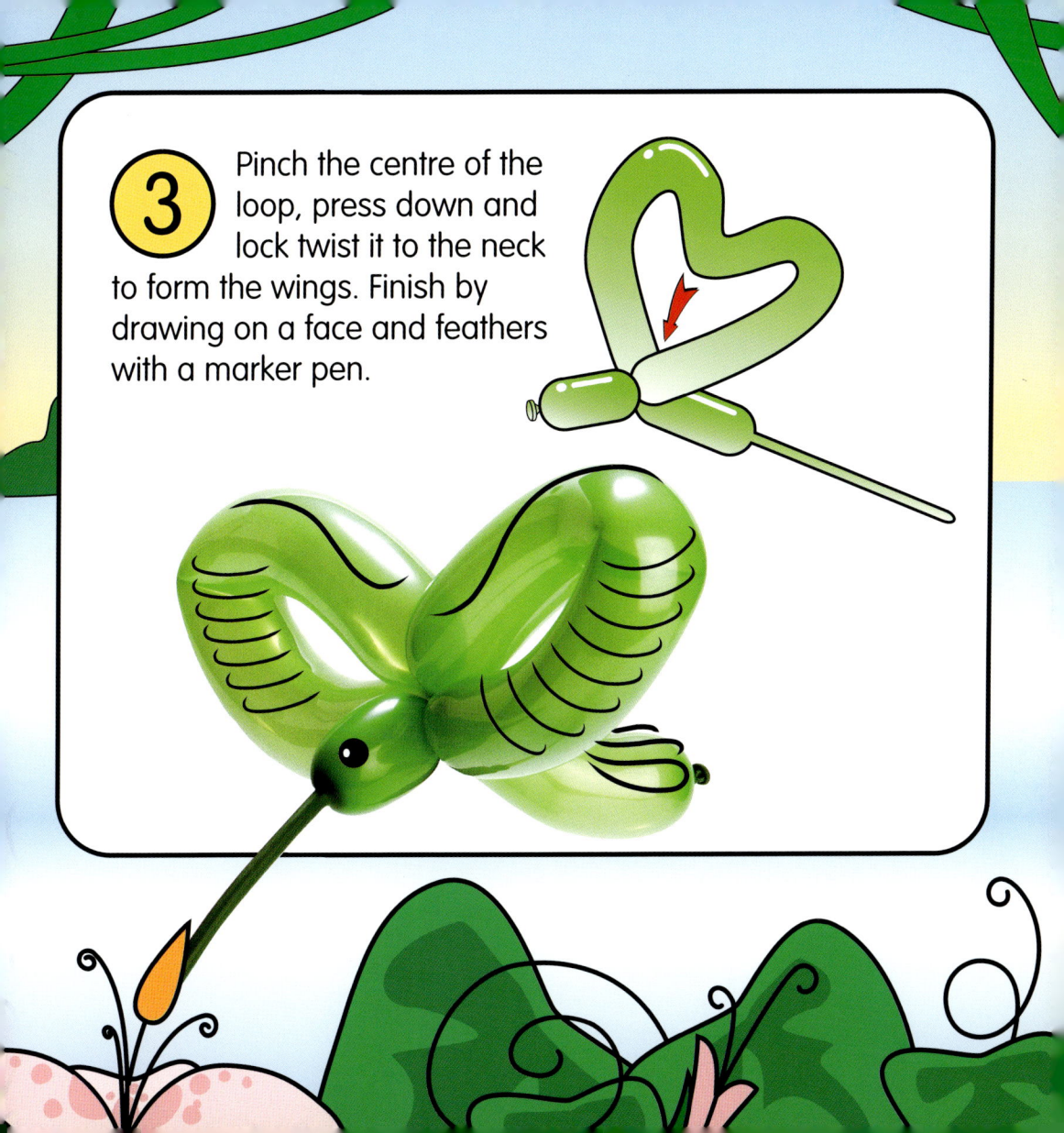

3 Pinch the centre of the loop, press down and lock twist it to the neck to form the wings. Finish by drawing on a face and feathers with a marker pen.

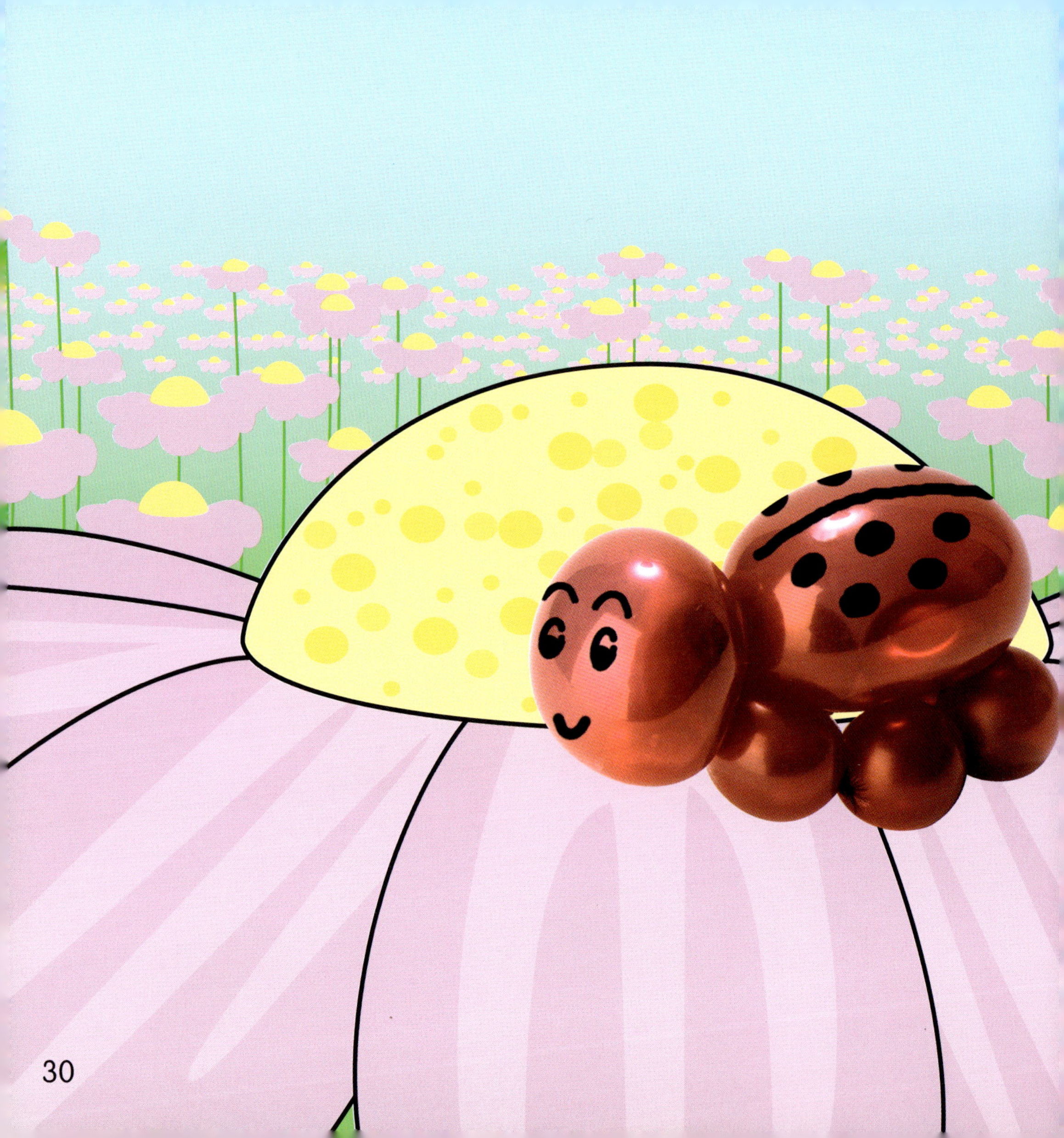

Lil Ladybird

You will need:
- one long balloon
- a marker pen

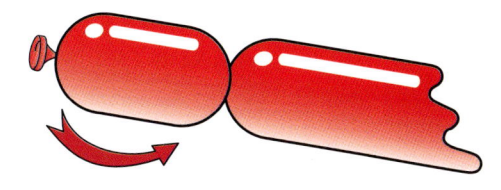

1 Inflate a single red balloon to about 25 cm and tie a knot in the end. Twist a 4 cm bubble and wrap the knot of the balloon into the twist to secure the bubble. This forms Lil's head.

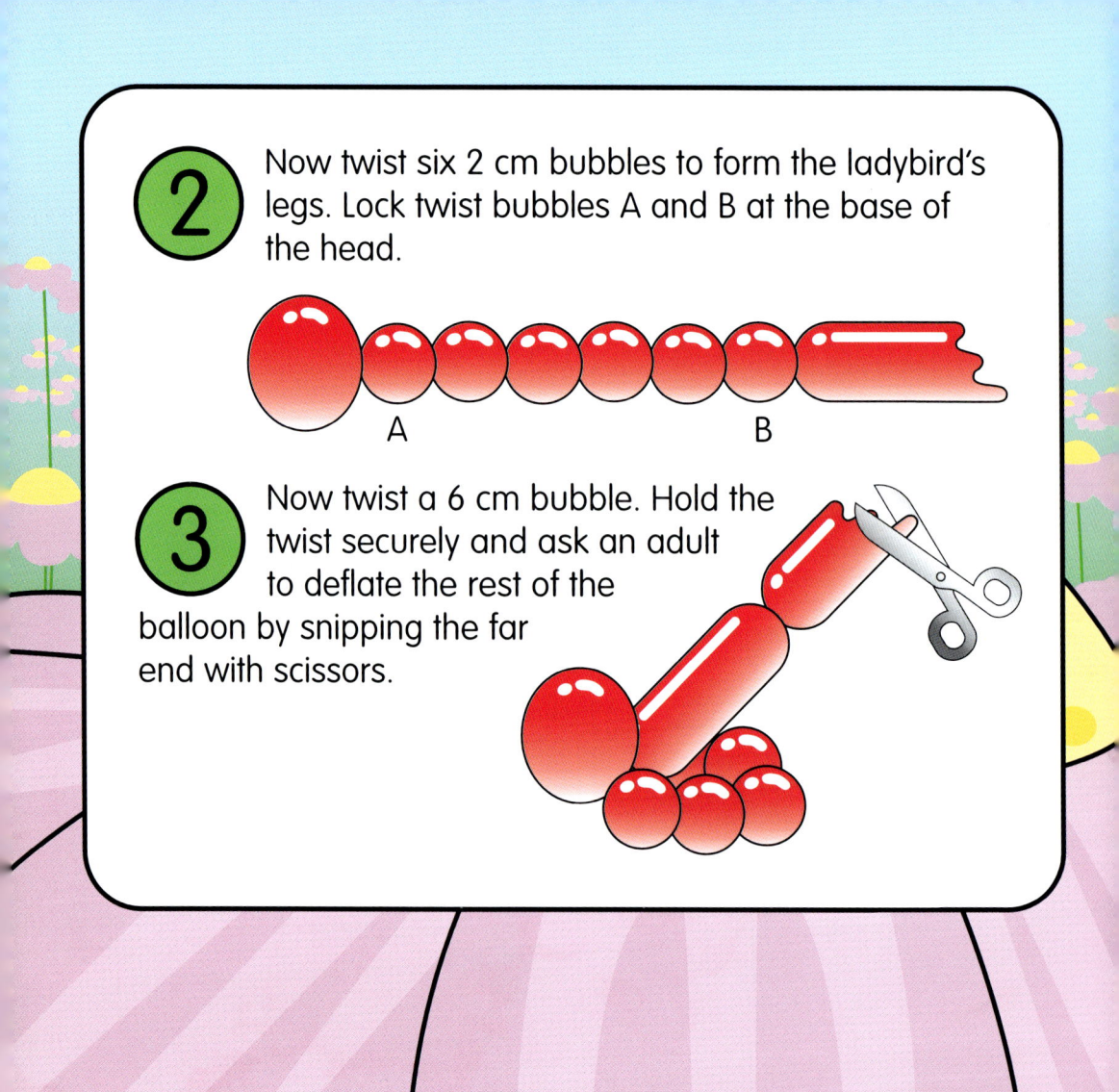

2 Now twist six 2 cm bubbles to form the ladybird's legs. Lock twist bubbles A and B at the base of the head.

A   B

3 Now twist a 6 cm bubble. Hold the twist securely and ask an adult to deflate the rest of the balloon by snipping the far end with scissors.

(4) Tie off the balloon at the last twist and ask an adult to cut off the deflated section. Wrap the knot between the two back legs to secure. This bubble is the ladybird's body.

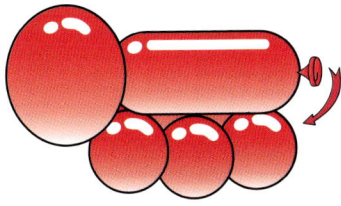

(5) Add cute little features to Lil's face with the marker pen. Don't forget the spots on her back!

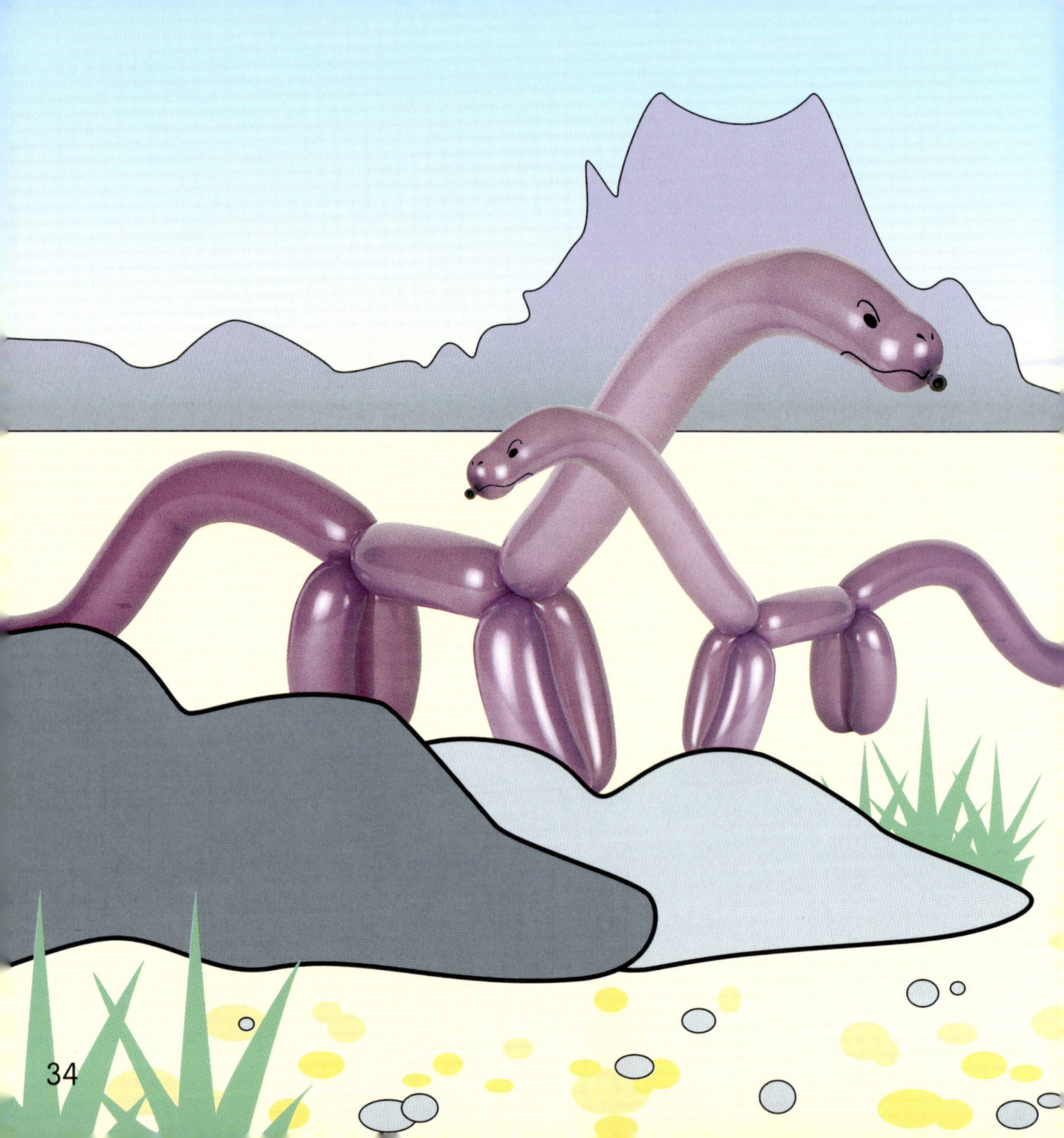

Barry Barosaurus

You will need:
- one long balloon
- a marker pen

1 Inflate the balloon to 80 cm and tie the end. Make a twist 30 cm from the knot and then two 8 cm twists. Lock twist the first and third twists together to make the front legs.

2 Make a twist 7 cm from the legs, then two more 8 cm twists. Lock twist the first and third twists together to form the back legs.

3 Line up both pairs of legs. Shape the remaining piece of balloon for the tail, and squeeze the neck to make it curve. Add a face with a marker pen.

38

Gary the Gastropod

You will need:
- one long balloon
- one balloon scrap
- sticker eyes

1 Inflate the balloon, leaving a 6 cm tip, and tie a knot in the end. From the knotted end, twist a 4 cm bubble and an 8 cm soft ear-twisted bubble.

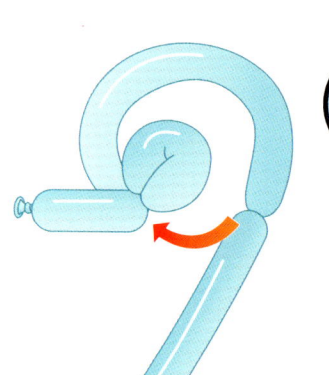

(2) Make a loop over this ear-twisted bubble and lock twist at the base, as shown.

(3) Make two soft 3 cm ear-twisted bubbles and position them on each side of the snail's shell that you have just made in step 2.

40

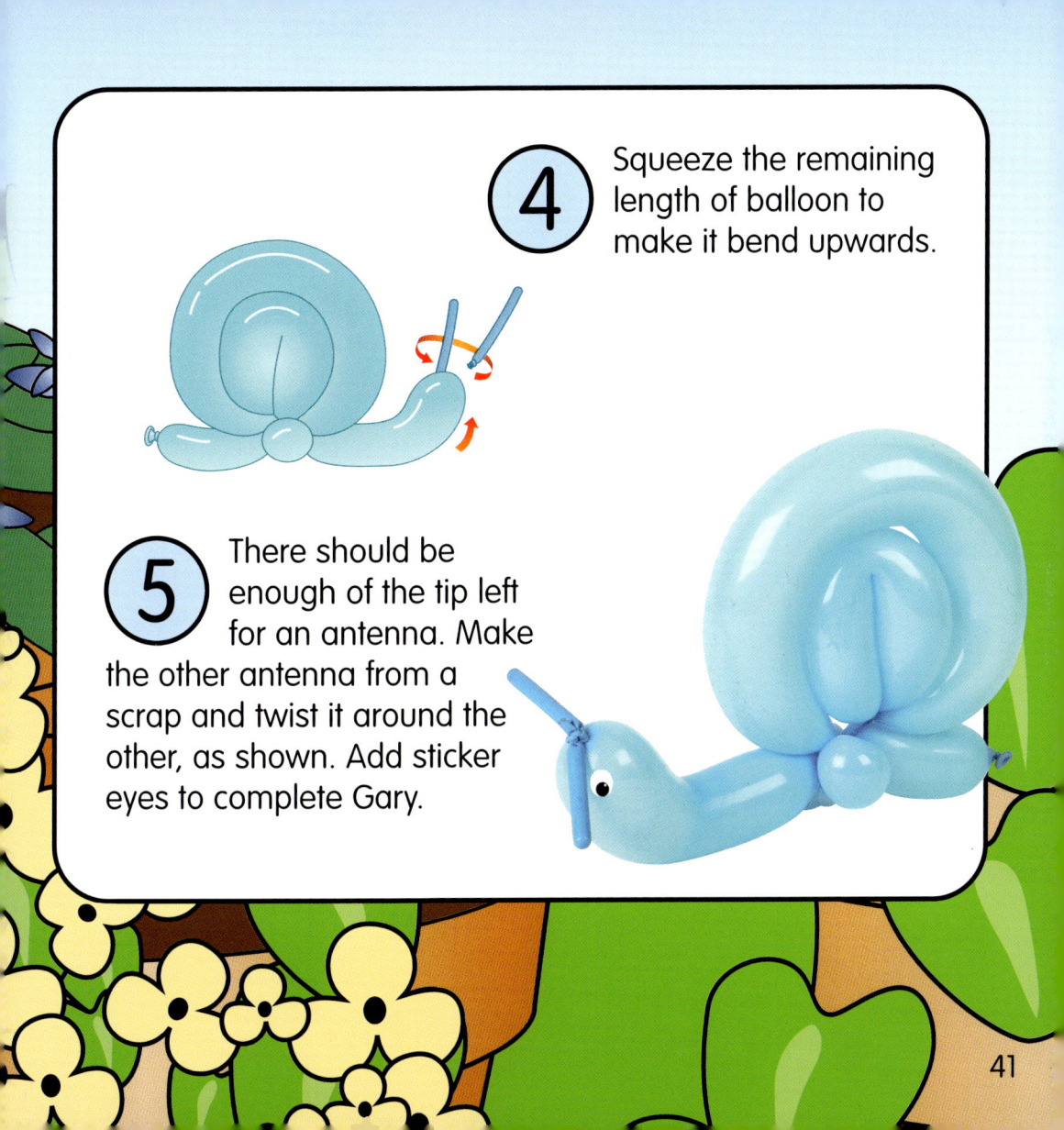

④ Squeeze the remaining length of balloon to make it bend upwards.

⑤ There should be enough of the tip left for an antenna. Make the other antenna from a scrap and twist it around the other, as shown. Add sticker eyes to complete Gary.

42

Serpent Stan

You will need:
- two long balloons
- one balloon scrap
- sticker eyes

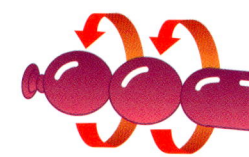

1 Inflate a long balloon, leaving a 6 cm tip. Make two 2 cm bubbles at the tied-off end.

(2) Next to these make a 10 cm bubble and ear twist to make a loop, as shown. Twist a 5 cm bubble. Then push it through the loop, as shown.

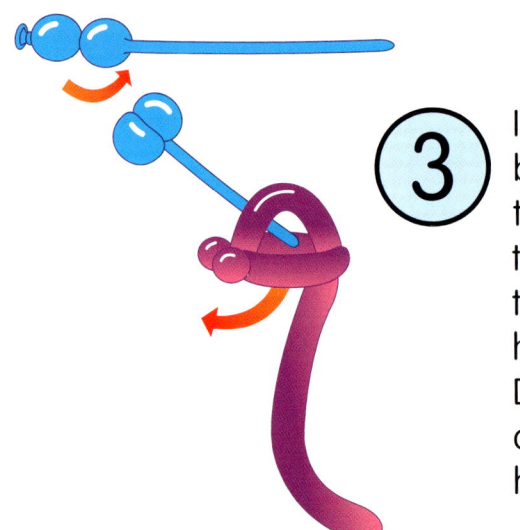

(3) Inflate a different coloured balloon to 4 cm, and make two 2 cm bubbles. Lock twist them together. Push these under the middle head bubble, as shown. Draw the remaining length of balloon down under the head to make a tongue.

(4) Using the balloon scrap, make a small bubble for the teeth. Attach, as shown. Stick on the eyes and, if you wish, draw on some scales using the marker pen.

45

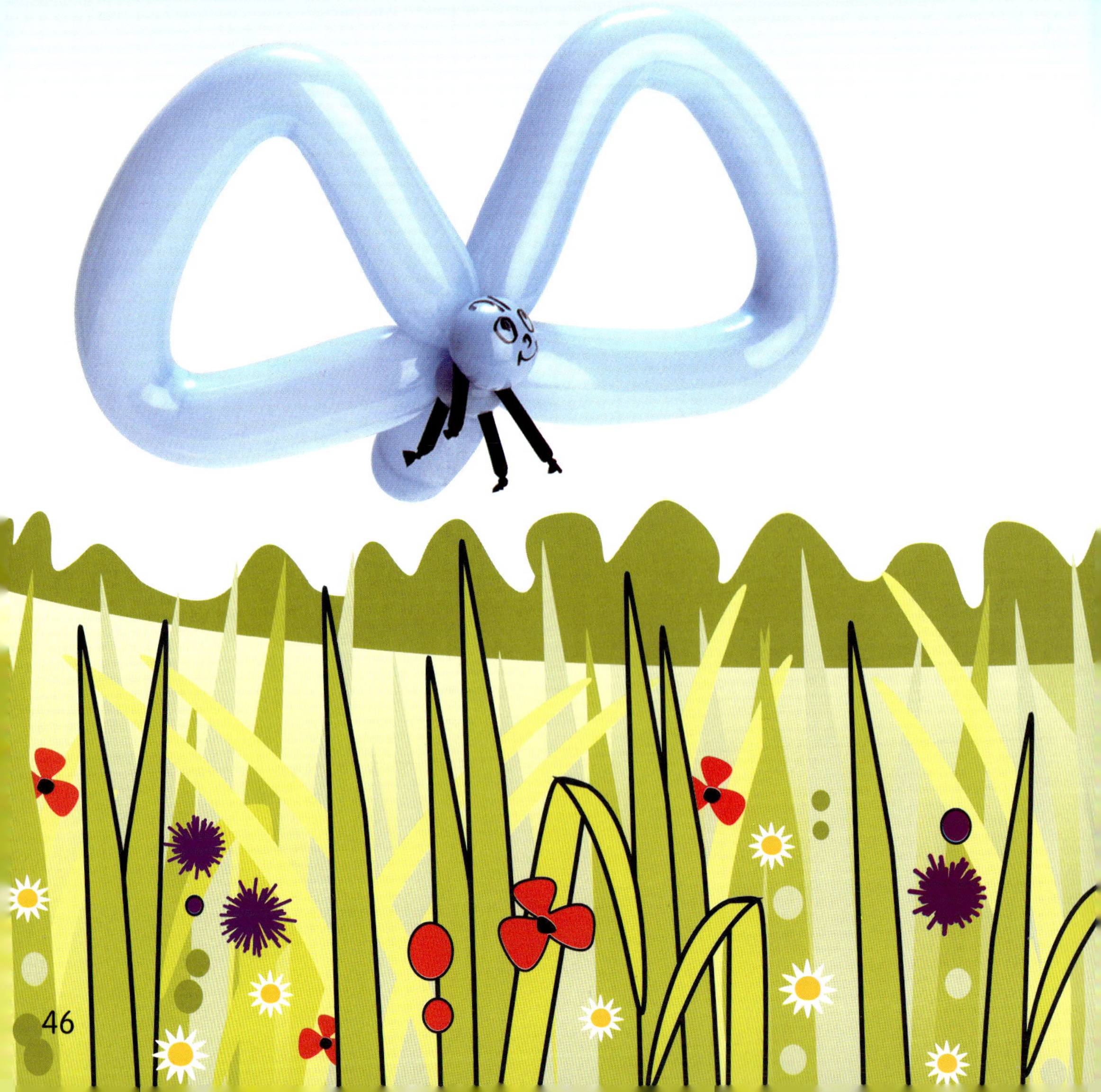

Flutterby!

You will need:
- one long balloon
- two balloon scraps
- a marker pen

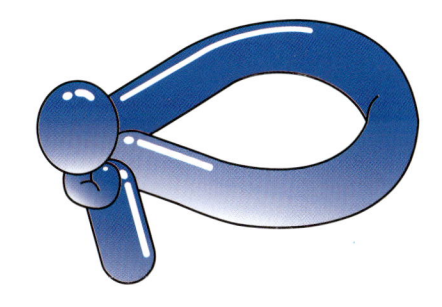

(1) Inflate the balloon but leave a 3 cm tip and tie the end. Make a 3 cm bubble to form the head. Twist a 5 cm bubble at the other end and lock twist it to the head. Ear twist a 2 cm bubble in this 5 cm bubble.

② Position this between the other two small bubbles to hold the body in line.

③ Find the centre of the large loop, opposite the last ear twist, and twist it in half (making a figure of eight) to make the wings. Shape each wing into an equal-sided triangle. Squeeze the angles gently to keep the wing in shape.

④ Make two sets of dangly legs with uninflated scraps. Fasten them in place on the body. Draw in a face to finish your beautiful butterfly!